Original Artwork © 1999 Debbie Mumm®
Mumm's The Word toll-free number 1-888-819-2923
or the web site: http://www.debbiemumm.com

Text © 1999 Brownlow Publishing Company
6309 Airport Freeway
Fort Worth, Texas 76117

ISBN: 1-57051-318-1

Cover/Interior: Koechel Peterson & Associates,
Minneapolis, MN

Printed in USA

TEA PARTY COOKBOOK

Illustrated by
DEBBIE MUMM

Recipes by
MAURA COOPER

Stories by
ROSA LINDA BUCHNER GRAZIANA

Brownlow

Recipe for a Special Friendship

TAKE two very special people,
sprinkle sunshine from above;
Add a cup of kindness
and a heaping spoonful of love.

A PINCH of sugar for sweetness,
rounds out the perfect measure;
Blend it all together
for a friendship sure to treasure!

CAKE

CHOWDER SOUP

CHICKEN

RECIPES

Table of Contents

Nutmeg Tea Cakes

Cake Ingredients

1 CUP ALL PURPOSE FLOUR

1 TSP. BAKING POWDER

2 TBS. UNSALTED BUTTER OR MARGARINE

1 TSP. FRESHLY GRATED NUTMEG

1/2 TSP. GROUND MACE

1/2 TSP. GROUND ALLSPICE

2 LARGE EGGS

1 CUP SUGAR

1/2 CUP MILK

COOKING SPRAY

Topping Ingredients

1 TBS. GROUND CINNAMON

1/2 TBS. GROUND NUTMEG

1 TBS. SUGAR

Preheat oven to 350 degrees. Spray a 9-inch by 9-inch by 2-inch baking pan with cooking spray. Combine flour, baking powder, salt, mace, allspice and freshly grated nutmeg in a bowl. In a small mixer bowl beat the eggs at high speed for 4 minutes or until thick. Gradually add in the sugar and beat on medium speed for 4 to 5 minutes or until the sugar dissolves. Add the dry ingredients to the egg mixture and stir until just combined. Combine the milk with the butter in a microwaveable bowl and microwave on high for 1 minute. Stir and make sure the butter is melted. Microwave another 30 seconds if necessary. Stir the hot milk and butter into the batter and mix well. Pour the batter into the prepared pan. Mix the cinnamon, ground nutmeg and sugar together and sprinkle over the top. Bake (at 350 degrees) for 20 to 25 minutes. Allow to cool slightly before cutting into squares.

Blessed are they who have the gift of making friends for it is one of God's best gifts.
THOMAS HUGHES

Walnut Muffins

1 3/4 cups all purpose flour

1/4 cup sugar

2 tsp. baking powder

1/2 tsp. salt

3 Tbs. finely ground walnuts

1/4 cup butter or margarine,
at room temperature

2 large eggs, slightly beaten

1 cup milk

12 walnut halves

Cooking spray

Preheat oven to 375 degrees. Spray a 12-cup muffin tin (2 1/2 inches each cup) with cooking spray. In a medium bowl combine the flour, sugar, baking powder, salt and ground walnuts and thoroughly combine. With pastry blender or two knives, cut in the butter or margarine till the mixture resembles coarse meal or crumbs. In a small bowl beat together the eggs and milk. Add the eggs and milk to the dry ingredients all at once and stir just until moistened.

Hint: Don't overmix; the batter should have a rough appearance.

Spoon the batter into the prepared muffin tin, filling each cup about 3/4 full. Place 1 walnut half on top of each cup and gently press into the batter. Bake (at 375 degrees) for 22 minutes until golden. Let muffins cool for 5 minutes in the tin before turning them out onto a wire rack.

Good Muffins, Best Mom

For just an instant when I taste that first delicious bite of Mom's home-baked muffins, I'm suddenly ten years old again, sitting with her at our kitchen table, sharing my first pot of tea, and having my first grown-up talk about boys.

I remember we chatted for a very long time that day, as we sipped our tea and taste-tested the muffin recipe she would become "famous" for. It was a day of firsts for both of us.

And as I so well remember, it was the day my mom first became my friend.

O taste and see
that the Lord is good!
PSALM 34:8

Chicken Salad Sandwiches

For the chicken salad:
Cut cooked white meat chicken into 1/4 inch dice.
Combine the cubed chicken with mayonnaise,
salt and pepper to taste and finely diced celery.

For the sandwiches:
Cut good quality white bread into thin slices.
Butter 1 side of each slice and remove the crusts.
Place a thin layer of chicken salad on 1 piece of buttered bread.
Put another slice on top, butter facing the chicken salad.
Cut on 2 diagonals in the shape of the letter X to produce
4 triangle-shaped finger sandwiches.

The greatest gift
you can give another
is to allow him to be himself.

Crunchy Oat Apricot Bars

1 3/4 cups all purpose flour

2 cups oats

1 cup packed dark brown sugar

1/2 tsp. ground cinnamon

2/3 cup margarine

1 1/2 tsp. vanilla extract

Cooking spray

1 1/2 cups apricot preserves

Preheat oven to 350 degrees. Lightly spoon flour into dry measuring cups and level with a knife. Place flour, oats, brown sugar, cinnamon, margarine and vanilla in a food processor and pulse 4 to 5 times till oat mixture resembles coarse meal. Coat a 13-inch by 9-inch pan with cooking spray. Press half of the oat mixture into the bottom of the pan. Spread apricot preserves over the oat mixture. Sprinkle remaining oat mixture over the preserves and press them in gently. Bake (at 350 degrees) for 35 minutes or until bubbly and golden. Cool completely on a wire rack, then cut into bars.

The supreme happiness of life is the conviction of being loved for yourself, or, more correctly, being loved in spite of yourself.

VICTOR HUGO

PURE VANILLA EXTRACT

8 OZ

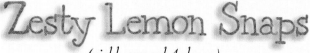

Zesty Lemon Snaps

(yield: around 4 dozen)

2 1/2 CUPS UNBLEACHED FLOUR

1 1/2 CUPS SUGAR

2 TSP. BAKING SODA

1/4 TSP. SALT

2 TBS. GRATED LEMON ZEST

(AROUND 3 VERY LARGE LEMONS)

1/2 CUP FRESHLY SQUEEZED LEMON JUICE

3/4 CUP CANOLA OIL

2 TSP. VANILLA EXTRACT

COOKING SPRAY

*HINT: Grate the lemon zest first before
squeezing the lemons for juice.*

Preheat the oven to 350 degrees. Combine all ingredients in a food processor or mixer and blend thoroughly. Spray a cookie sheet with cooking spray. Drop the batter by teaspoonfuls onto the prepared cookie sheet about 2 inches apart. Bake (at 350 degrees) for 12 minutes or until the edges of the cookies are golden. Cool on racks. Repeat this process until all cookies are baked.

Give what you have. To someone
it may be better than you dare to think.

HENRY WADSWORTH LONGFELLOW

Cucumber Sandwiches

Hint: Use country-style white bread.

Cut good quality white bread into thin slices. Butter one side of each slice and remove the crusts. Thinly slice seedless (hot house or European) cucumbers and place one layer of slices on 1 piece of buttered bread. Put another slice on top, butter facing the cucumbers. Cut on 2 diagonals in the shape of the letter X to produce 4 triangle-shaped finger sandwiches.

There can be no unity,
no delight of love,
no harmony, no good in being,
where there is but one.
Two at least are needed
for oneness.

GEORGE MACDONALD

It Wasn't the Tea

Now my "garden club" is a little different from most. This is just a group of girls who love flowers, tea and each other. We have no dues, no programs and no rules. The club meets whenever we want to.

Last Saturday, we were supposed to have a tea luncheon and exchange our favorite flowers. It would have been delightful.

Instead, we spent the day helping a sick friend. Her house was a mess. Her children were out of clean clothes. Her kitchen sink had more dirty dishes than I have ever seen at one time. We cleaned, scrubbed, or washed anything or anybody we could grab.

When we finally stopped for a break, all we could find was a jar of instant tea in the back of the pantry. To complete the experience, we got out the good china cups and toasted our tea cups as we ate some banana bread I had brought from home. We decided it was the best tea party we have ever had, but somehow I'm not sure the tea had much to do with it.

Lemon Blueberry Pound Cake

Cooking spray

1 Tbs. all purpose flour

1 (18.25 oz) package yellow cake mix with pudding

1/3 cup lemon juice

1 tsp. vanilla extract

1 8 oz. package cream cheese, room temp.
(reduced fat is OK)

3 large egg whites

1 large egg

1 1/2 cups fresh blueberries or
frozen blueberries, thawed

1 cup sifted powdered sugar

4 tsp. lemon juice

Nothing but Heaven itself is better than a friend
who is really a friend.

Preheat oven to 350 degrees. Coat a 12-cup Bundt pan with cooking spray, then dust with 1 Tbs. flour and remove any excess. Combine cake mix, 1/3 cup lemon juice, vanilla, cream cheese, egg whites and whole egg in a large bowl. Beat with a mixer on low speed for 30 seconds. Beat with a mixer on medium speed for 2 minutes. Fold in the blueberries. Pour cake batter into the prepared pan. Bake (at 350 degrees) for 50 minutes or until a wooden toothpick inserted in the center comes out clean. Cool the cake for 10 minutes before removing it from its pan. Cool the cake completely on a wire rack. Combine the sugar and 4 tsp. lemon juice in a small bowl and drizzle the glaze over the cooled cake.

Yummy Banana Bread

1 2/3 cups all purpose flour

1 tsp. baking soda 🐝 1/2 tsp. salt

1 scant cup sugar

1/3 cup canola oil

2 large eggs, lightly beaten

3 very ripe bananas, mashed

1/2 cup sour cream

1 tsp. vanilla extract

1/2 cup chopped walnuts

FLOUR

SUGAR

TEA

Preheat oven to 350 degrees. Grease and flour bottom only of a 5-inch by 9-inch loaf pan. Combine flour, baking soda, salt and sugar thoroughly. Add in oil, eggs, mashed bananas, sour cream and vanilla and blend well. Fold in nuts. Pour mixture into the prepared loaf pan. Bake for 1 hour and 15 minutes. Cool in loaf pan for 5 minutes before removing to a wire rack. Cool completely before slicing.

Serve one another in love.

GALATIANS 5:13

Grandma's Kisses and Cookies

As I sat in her front room on the slip-covered sofa sobbing over my scraped but now-bandaged knee, Grandma softly spoke kind and comforting words. She smothered me with lots of hugs and kisses while soothing Darjeeling brewed on the teacart—right next to a dish stacked high with oatmeal Toll-house cookies.

Gently she lifted the delicate hand-painted teapot and started to pour when, suddenly, soft beautiful chimes began playing "Tea for Two," filling every cozy corner of the room with song.

Grandma's musical teapot had made me feel so very special that afternoon. Yes, there was music and tea, but what I remember most was the love.

Grandma's Chocolate Cookies

(yield: around 2 dozen)

1 BOX DEVIL'S FOOD CAKE MIX
6 OUNCES SEMISWEET CHOCOLATE CHIPS
1/2 CUP CANOLA OIL
2 LARGE EGGS

Preheat oven to 350 degrees. Combine all ingredients
in a large bowl. Beat with an electric mixer until blended.
Drop onto an ungreased cookie sheet by rounded
teaspoonfuls, 2 1/2 inches
apart. Bake 10 minutes,
then remove cookie sheets
from the oven. Allow the
cookies to rest on the baking
sheets for 5 minutes. Remove
the cookies with a thin,
flexible spatula to a wire
rack to cool completely.

Strawberry Gems

2 CUPS FLOUR

2 STICKS (8 OUNCES TOTAL) OF UNSALTED BUTTER,
(ROOM TEMPERATURE)

2 EGG YOLKS

1 TSP. VANILLA

3/4 CUP PACKED DARK BROWN SUGAR

10 OUNCES STRAWBERRY PRESERVES

1/2 CUP CHOPPED PECANS

COOKING SPRAY

Preheat oven to 350 degrees. Thoroughly combine flour, butter, egg yolks, vanilla and brown sugar. Spray a 9-inch by 13-inch baking pan with cooking spray. Press the mixture into the prepared baking pan, trying to keep an even thickness. Spread the strawberry preserves on top. Sprinkle with chopped pecans, gently pressing them in. Bake (at 350 degrees) for 30 to 35 minutes. Let it cool in the pan completely before cutting into squares.

Once in an age, God sends to some of us a friend
who loves in us not the person that we are,
but the angel we may be.

HARRIET BEECHER STOWE

Molasses Crinkles

(yield: around 5 dozen)

1 1/2 CUPS UNSALTED BUTTER (12 OUNCES),
(AT ROOM TEMPERATURE)

2 CUPS PACKED DARK BROWN SUGAR

2 LARGE EGGS, LIGHTLY BEATEN

1/2 CUP MOLASSES

4 1/2 CUPS FLOUR

4 TSP. BAKING SODA

1/2 TSP. SALT

1 TSP. GROUND CLOVES

2 TSP. GROUND CINNAMON

2 TSP. GROUND GINGER

GRANULATED SUGAR (AROUND 1/2 CUP)

Combine the butter, brown sugar, eggs and molasses in a large bowl. In a separate bowl, thoroughly mix together the flour, baking soda, salt, cloves, cinnamon and ginger. Mix the dry ingredients into the wet ones to make the dough. Refrigerate the dough for at least 1 hour. Preheat the oven to 375 degrees. Take out the dough a tablespoon at a time and shape it into a ball. Roll the tops in granulated sugar. Repeat the following process until all cookies are baked. Place the dough balls (sugar facing up) on an ungreased cookie sheet, 2 inches apart. Sprinkle 1 or 2 drops of water on each one. Bake (at 375 degrees) for 8 to 10 minutes. Cool on a wire rack.

The only people with whom we should try to get even are those who have helped us.
MAE MALOO

PURE MOLASSES

8 OZ

Samantha's Cupcakes

Last October I volunteered to bake for my daughter's preschool Pumpkin Party, unaware that a new classmate had joined the morning group. As was the custom, the "baker's" child had the honor of distributing the goodies, so I watched as Samantha methodically handed out our orange-glazed candy-corn topped cupcakes.

I will never forget the sadness that filled her big, brown eyes when Samantha realized she would have to

It is one mark of a friend
that she makes you wish
to be at your best
while you are with her.

HENRY VAN DYKE

do without, as we were one cupcake short.
Just then the new girl, Debby, held out her
own cupcake and shyly asked,
"Want some of mine?"

It was the beginning of a beautiful friendship
for the two girls. It also reminded me of how
powerful simple kindness can be.

Be kind and compassionate
to one another.
EPHESIANS 4:32

Cranberry Nut Bread

2 CUPS ALL PURPOSE FLOUR ✳ 1 TSP. SALT

1 1/2 TSP. BAKING POWDER ✳ 1/2 TSP. BAKING SODA

1 CUP SUGAR ✳ 1 LARGE EGG, LIGHTLY BEATEN

2 TBS. UNSALTED BUTTER, MELTED ✳ 2 TBS. HOT WATER

1/2 CUP ORANGE JUICE ✳ GRATED RIND OF 1 ORANGE

1 CUP RAW CRANBERRIES, CUT IN HALVES

1/2 CUP CHOPPED PECANS

Preheat oven to 325 degrees. Sift together flour, salt, baking powder, baking soda and sugar. Add egg, melted butter, hot water, orange juice and orange rind. Stir until well mixed, but do not beat. Stir in cranberries and nuts. Grease and flour a 5-inch by 9-inch loaf pan. Pour mixture into the loaf pan and bake (at 325 degrees) for 1 hour. Check for doneness by inserting a toothpick into the middle of the bread. If it comes out wet, bake for another 10 minutes. Remove the loaf from its pan and, while hot, wrap in aluminum foil. Store immediately in the refrigerator for 24 hours.

Life is partly what we make it, and partly what it is made by the friends whom we choose.

TEHYI HSIEH

Apple Spice Cake

1 STICK MARGARINE 🍎 1/2 CUP SOLID SHORTENING

2 CUPS SUGAR 🍎 4 LARGE EGGS, BEATEN

2 CUPS FLOUR 🍎 2 TSP. GROUND CINNAMON

1/4 TSP. GROUND CLOVES 🍎 1/2 TSP. GROUND NUTMEG

1 TSP. BAKING SODA 🍎 1 TSP. SALT

5 CUPS PEELED AND CORED CHOPPED APPLES

1 CUP CHOPPED PECANS

1 CUP SEEDLESS RAISINS

Preheat oven to 350 degrees. Grease and flour a Bundt pan. Cream together margarine, shortening and sugar. Add in eggs and mix until fluffy. Mix in flour, cinnamon, cloves, nutmeg, baking soda and salt. The batter will be very creamy. Fold in apple chunks, pecans and raisins. Pour into the prepared pan and bake for 40 minutes (at 350 degrees). Remove cake from pan and let it cool completely on a wire rack. Sprinkle with powdered sugar.

The friendships which last are those wherein each friend respects the other's dignity to the point of not really wanting anything from him.

CYRIL CONNOLLY

ZUCCHINI BREAD

(yield: two loaves)

3 LARGE EGGS, LIGHTLY BEATEN ✳ 1 CUP CANOLA OIL

1 TBS. VANILLA EXTRACT ✳ 2 CUPS SUGAR

2 CUPS PEELED, GRATED RAW ZUCCHINI ✳ 1 TSP. BAKING SODA

1 TBS. GROUND CINNAMON ✳ 3 CUPS ALL PURPOSE FLOUR

1 TSP. SALT ✳ 1/4 TSP. BAKING POWDER

1 CUP PECAN PIECES ✳ COOKING SPRAY

Preheat oven to 350 degrees. Spray 2 loaf pans, approximately 5-inches by 9-inches each. In a large bowl combine eggs, oil, vanilla, sugar and grated zucchini. Sift together the baking soda, cinnamon, flour, salt and baking powder. Mix dry ingredients together with wet ingredients. Fold in nuts. Divide the batter evenly between the two loaf pans. Bake (350 degrees) for one hour or until a toothpick inserted in the middle comes out clean.

THAT BOY

On a sweltering July day some time ago, while struggling
with the iced tea stand I "built," Jimmy passed by and offered his
help. Now Jimmy was "The Boy I Had My Eye On,"
and together we propped the makeshift peddler's stand against
the white picket fence surrounding my front yard.

With butterflies dancing in my stomach, I poured Jimmy a glass
of the cool refreshing drink to say thanks, secretly hoping he
would stay awhile. We talked all through the hot afternoon
and discovered we liked many of the same things—including
how we preferred our iced tea: sweet and lemony.

I still melt quicker than ice cubes for that boy.
But now he tells our daughters some wild story of how
I used a glass of tea to catch him. How preposterous!

Walnut Lace Cookies

(yield: around 4 dozen)

1 1/2 CUPS FIRMLY PACKED DARK BROWN SUGAR

1/2 CUP SOLID SHORTENING

1/4 CUP UNSALTED BUTTER, AT ROOM TEMPERATURE

1 LARGE EGG ✳ 1 TSP. VANILLA EXTRACT

1 1/2 CUPS ALL PURPOSE FLOUR

1/2 TSP. SALT

1 CUP WALNUTS, FINELY CHOPPED

COOKING SPRAY

Preheat oven to 375 degrees. Lightly spray a cookie sheet with cooking spray. Combine brown sugar, shortening and butter in a large bowl. Beat at medium speed of mixer until creamy. Add in egg and vanilla. Beat until light and fluffy. Add in flour, salt and nuts. Stir until well blended. Repeat the following process until all cookies are baked. Shape level tablespoonfuls of dough into balls and place them on the prepared cookie sheet 1-inch apart. Flatten each one to 1/8 inch thickness on the baking sheet. Bake (at 375 degrees) for 7 to 8 minutes or until edges are golden. Cool on baking sheet for 2 minutes. Remove to a wire rack.

We are knit together
by strong ties of love.
COLOSSIANS 2:2

Creamed Scones

2 1/2 cups all purpose flour

5 tsp. baking powder

5 Tbs. sugar

3 Tbs. chilled unsalted butter,
(cut into small pieces)

1/2 cup milk

1/4 cup whipping cream

1 egg yolk

Cooking spray

Flour for the work surface

1 large egg, beaten to blend
(for the glaze)

Unsalted butter

Raspberry preserves and
Sweet orange marmalade

Queen's Jam

Preheat the oven to 450 degrees. Lightly spray a heavy, large cookie sheet with cooking spray. Sift together flour and baking powder into a medium bowl. Mix in sugar. Add the butter and rub between your fingers until the mixture resembles fine meal. Pour the milk, whipping cream and egg yolk into a small bowl and blend with a whisk. Add the wet to the dry ingredients and stir just until combined. Turn the dough out onto a floured work surface and press to a thickness of 1 inch. Cut out rounds using a 2-inch or 2 1/2-inch cookie cutter or biscuit cutter.

Gather together the scraps and press them together to a thickness of 1 inch and continue to cut out rounds. Place the rounds on the prepared cookie sheet, spacing them apart evenly so none are touching. Brush the tops with the glaze (beaten egg). Bake (at 450 degrees) until golden brown, around 15 minutes. Transfer scones to a wire rack to cool slightly. Serve with butter, preserves or marmalade.

Hint: Break open the scones gently with fingers, not a knife, for the perfect texture to receive the butter, etc.

The Giggle Girls

We laughed so often we were dubbed The Giggle Girls. Once when playing "house guest" on my back porch we simultaneously asked, "More Tea?" while reaching for the teapot. Linda and I once again lived up to our nickname.

With pinkies out, we would pretend to be grownup and playfully sip our Friendship Tea, this is how we bonded. With *pinkies swear*, we turned every incidental bit of news and gossip into a sacred secret, we two shared only by us. The back porch of my childhood brewed more than a perfect blend of tea—it brewed a perfect blend of friendship. We Giggle Girls are just a "little" older now, but we have so much to treasure.

A cheerful heart
is good medicine.
PROVERBS 17:22

Watercress Sandwiches

Hint: Use country-style white bread.

Cut good quality white bread into thin slices.
Butter 1 side of each slice and remove the crusts.
Thoroughly rinse, dry, and remove the stems
from a bunch of watercress. Place 1 layer of leaves
on 1 piece of buttered bread. Put another slice on top,
butter facing the watercress. Cut 2 diagonals
in the shape of the letter X to produce
4 triangle-shaped finger sandwiches.

Happy is the house
that shelters a friend.
R.W.E.

Mamaw's Carrot Cake

Cooking spray

1 cup pitted prunes ✳ 1/3 cup water

3 cups all purpose flour

1 cup sugar

2 tsp. ground cinnamon

2 tsp. baking soda

1 tsp. baking powder ✳ 1 tsp. salt

1/2 tsp. ground ginger

1 (8 ounce) container plain nonfat yogurt

1 (8 ounce) container frozen no-cholesterol
egg substitute, thawed

3/4 cup packed light brown sugar

1/4 cup canola oil ✳ 1 tsp. vanilla extract

2 cups lightly packed shredded carrots
(about 3 medium size carrots)

Preheat oven to 350 degrees. Spray a 9-inch by 13-inch glass baking dish with oil. In a small saucepan simmer the prunes and water, uncovered, over medium heat, till the prunes are very soft and the water evaporates. Keep stirring and mashing the prunes until they're smooth. In a large bowl combine the flour, sugar, cinnamon, baking soda, baking powder, salt and ginger. In a medium bowl, beat together with a wire whisk or fork the yogurt, egg substitute, brown sugar, oil and vanilla until smooth. Stir in the shredded carrots and puréed prunes into the medium bowl with the wet ingredients. Stir the carrot mixture into the large bowl with the dry ingredients just until the flour is moistened. Pour batter into the prepared dish. Bake (at 350 degrees) for 30 to 35 minutes or until a toothpick inserted in the center of the cake comes out clean. Cool cake in its pan on a wire rack.

For memory has painted this perfect day
With colors that never fade,
And we find at the end of a perfect day
The soul of a friend we've made.
O. HENRY

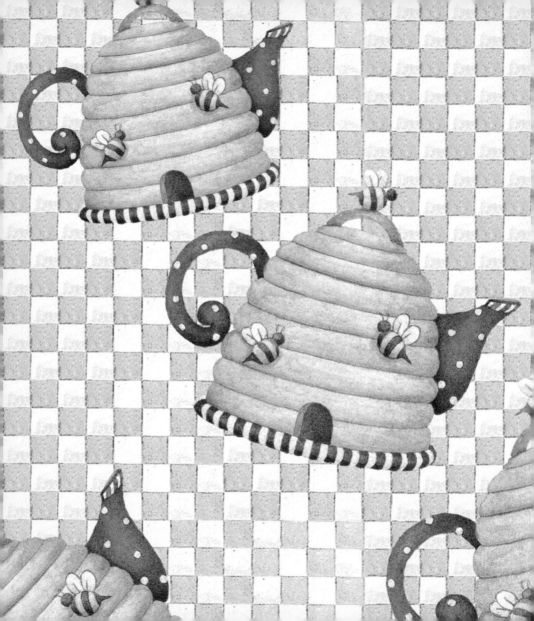